BEARCUB BIOS

MEGAN RAPINOE

SOCCER SUPERSTAR

by Rachel Rose

Consultant: Beth Gambro
Reading Specialist, Yorkville, Illinois

BEARPORT PUBLISHING

Minneapolis, Minnesota

Teaching Tips

BEFORE READING

- Discuss what a biography is. What kinds of things might a biography tell a reader?
- Look through the glossary together. Read and discuss the words.
- Go on a picture walk, looking through the pictures to discuss vocabulary and make predictions about the text.

DURING READING

- Encourage readers to point to each word as it is read. Stop occasionally to ask readers to point to a specific word in the text.
- If a reader encounters an unknown word, ask them to look at the rest of the page. Are there any clues to help them understand?

AFTER READING

- Check for understanding.
  - Where did Megan Rapinoe grow up?
  - What does she do?
  - What does she care about?
- Ask the readers to think deeper.
  - If you met Megan, what question would you like to ask her? Why?

Credits:
Cover, © Romain Biard/Shutterstock; Title page, © Romain Biard/Shutterstock; 3, © lev radin/Shutterstock; 5, © Jose Breton- Pics Action/Shutterstock; 7, © ZUMA Press Inc/Alamy Stock Photo; 9, © Michael Regan/Getty Images; 10-11, © ZUMA Press/Alamy Stock Photo; 12-13, © A.PAES/Shutterstock; 14, © jan kranendonk/Shutterstock; 17, © WENN Rights Ltd/Alamy Stock Photo; 18-19, © Ethan Miller/Getty Images; 20-21, © JASON CONNOLLY/Getty Images; 22, © Jose Breton-Pics Action/Shutterstock; 23TL, © Tom Merton/iStock; 23TR, © MarijaRadovic/iStock; 23BL, © Romain Biard/Shutterstock; and 23BR, © lazyllama/Shutterstock.

Library of Congress Cataloging-in-Publication Data

Names: Rose, Rachel, 1968– author. | Bearport Publishing. Title: Megan Rapinoe : soccer superstar / by Rachel Rose. Description: Bearcub Books Edition. | Minneapolis, Minnesota : Bearport Publishing Company, 2020. | Series: Bearcub Bios | Includes webography. | Includes bibliographical references and index. Identifiers: LCCN 2019060287 (print) | LCCN 2019060288 (ebook) | ISBN 9781642809800 (Library Binding) | ISBN 9781642809916 (Paperback) | ISBN 9781647470029 (eBook) Subjects: LCSH: Rapinoe, Megan, 1985–Juvenile literature. | Women soccer players—United States—Biography—Juvenile literature. | Soccer players—United States—Biography—Juvenile literature. | Women athletes—United States—Biography—Juvenile literature. | Political activists—United States—Biography—Juvenile literature. Classification: LCC GV942.7.R366 R67 2020 (print) | LCC GV942.7.R366 (ebook) | DDC 796.334092 [B]—dc23 LC record available at https://lccn.loc.gov/2019060287 LC ebook record available at https://lccn.loc.gov/2019060288

For more information, write to Bearport Publishing, 5357 Penn Avenue South, Minneapolis, MN 55419.

Printed in the United States of America.

Contents

Top Player

It was the 2019 Women's World Cup.

Megan Rapinoe scored!

She helped the U.S. team win the game.

Megan's Life

Megan grew up in California.

She has five brothers and sisters.

Megan started playing soccer when she was four.

Megan with her parents

Megan played soccer in college.

She also played for the U.S. team.

In 2012, she won a gold medal at the **Olympics**.

Megan in 2012

PROVIDENCE
Health & Services
modo
15

Megan has played for many teams.

Today, she plays on the Reign FC team.

She still plays for the U.S. team, too.

Megan and her twin sister work together.

They teach kids soccer.

A Street Football World game

Megan helps kids around the world.

She works with the group Street Football World.

Megan believes soccer can make lives better.

In 2012, Megan told the world she is **gay**.

She wants to stand up for people.

She wants what is fair for everyone.

Pride
Leadership
Service
Megan Rapinoe
Board of Directors Award

Megan's girlfriend is named Sue.

Sue is a basketball player.

Sue also works to help kids.

Sue
Megan

People know Megan.

She wants to use her **fame** to help people.

And she will keep playing the game she loves.

Did You Know?

Born: July 5, 1985

Family: Denise (mother), Jim (father), CeCe (sister), Jennifer (sister), Rachael (sister), Michael (brother), Brian (brother)

When she was a kid: Megan wore a **jersey** with the number seven.

Special fact: Megan's twin sister was born 11 minutes before her.

Megan says: "It's our responsibility to make this world a better place."

Life Connections

Megan shows the world who she is. She believes in helping people. What do you believe in?

Glossary

fame being well known

gay a person who likes people of the same sex

jersey the shirt worn by a member of a sports team

Olympics a world sports contest held every four years

Index

Read More

Adamson, Thomas K. *Soccer (Blastoff! Readers: Let's Play Sports!).* Minneapolis: Bellwether (2020).

Sherman, Jill. *Megan Rapinoe (Pro Sport Biographies).* Mankato, MN: Amicus (2020).

Learn More Online

1. Go to **www.factsurfer.com**
2. Enter "**Megan Rapinoe**" into the search box.
3. Click on the cover of this book to see a list of websites.

About the Author

Rachel Rose lives in San Francisco. She grew up in Ireland, where soccer is very popular. In Ireland, it is called football.